God Loves A Poet

By
James T. Huckleberry

Airleaf
Publishing

airleaf.com

ISBN: 1-59453-751-8

Dedication

This work is dedicated to the poem in all of us.

God Loves A Poet

What the hand writes
Is of heart and soul
Be it depths of darkness
Or heights of hope.

It is the courage
And truth of a poet
That is pleasing to God
Who reads every line.

James T. Huckleberry
19 February 2005

Introduction

Heart and soul is who you are. The most critical element of a poem is truthfulness. Truth is not a popular choice so expect rejection. Be content to have your poem published. Many will share your deepest thoughts and inner feelings.

Poetic Selections

Featured Poems

Poems, in this section, are recent works which have been individually selected and published as part of a compilation of poems.

A SONNET TO GOD

You are my soul
i desire to serve.
life without You
is horrible death.
i am weak.
i am a sinner,
and i am afraid.
i truly need You,
for evil it seems
encircles my dreams.

on darkest day
and loneliest hour,
i pray Your Name
never leaves my lips.

ON THE WINGS OF POETRY, Famous Poets Press, 2004

MORAL VALUES

The world was stunned
When an election was won
By the vote of free people
Of every race and religion.

We are a nation of hope
Drawn to the end of a rope
By overt acts of immorality
That overwhelmed our senses.

Beheading innocent people
Shook our white-washed steeples.
Legalizing same sex marriage
Caused our pot to over boil.

We are a nation of faith
And God is in our soil.

INVOKING THE MUSE, The International Library of Poetry, 2004

GAY MARRIAGE

Man with man,
Woman with woman,
Is mutual self love
Without a child.

Think about it,
No created life,
Who then becomes
Endangered species?

Is darkness light?
Is light a darkness?
Is evil good
And goodness evil?

Unnatural, unholy,
It won't be long,
Before God's children
Are truly gone.

Soon to be published by Noble House

HOW MANY NAILS

Today gay marriage is legal
In the State of Massachusetts.
Yesterday at Abu Ghraib
We lost faith and personal honor.
Tomorrow God will be removed
From history books and public places.
How many nails will it take
To seal our nation's coffin?

THE INTERNATIONAL WHO'S WHO IN POETRY,
The International Library of Poetry, 2004

A STRANGE SONNET

You drove on a highway I paved today.
I processed a loan on your new home.
I've plowed your road in the fury of winter,
Delivered your mail and served you dinner.

We've sat side by side at all the games.
We've heard the names of our sons and daughters.
We casually say as we browse the paper,
"I know that person, I think he's our neighbor."

Having met many times is it not strange,
We vaguely remember each other's name.
Both in life's stream, shallow it seems,
Our paths never shared each other's dream.

You depend on me and I upon you,
Is it not strange we're strangers too.

THE COLORS OF LIFE, The International Library of Poetry, 2003

WHAT LIVES IF NOT OUR SOUL

Our body sustains enormous physical punishment,
Continually abused, by us or others, it will fail.
Our mind withstands tremendous anguish and pain,
Fried or out of control, it also withers and dies.
What lives if not our soul, created in God's image,
The essence of our total existence and being.

No ungodly creature, crawling on earth or hell,
Can destroy what God has already given us.
If our soul is not an absolute truth, where do we go?
When we're all spaced out and lost at sea.
If our soul is not an absolute truth, what do we do?
When faced with mortal or eminent danger.

What lives if not our soul, created in God's image,
Long after the body and mind have gone.

COLOURS OF THE HEART, Noble House Publishers, 2004

WINTER OF FEAR

Bleak is winter this season.
Is eminent war the reason,
Or is it a terrorist attack
Weighing heavily on our back?

America take no chances.
Evil sits on barren branches,
Poised to strike at will,
Waiting for a massive kill.

Christians prepare for battle.
Let others tend to goats and cattle.
Satan's real make no mistake,
Keep your faith and souls awake.

This is a winter of fear.
Chill of it all grows ever near.
Our lambs are in a desert sand,
Time has come to pray and stand.

THEATRE OF THE MIND, Noble House Publishers, 2003

MAY GOD LIVE IN AMERICA AGAIN

Satan's assassins
In an act of treachery
Walked through gaping holes
In America's spiritual foundation
And wounded our hearts.

Hearts in the brine
Of earthly pleasures.
Transgressing hearts
Tuned out to God,
His Son and Holy Spirit.

On September Eleventh
Without God's protection,
Evil crept in
And killed in an instant
Family, neighbors and friends.

Our tears and prayers
Are not business as usual.
Our tears and prayers
Reach out to Jesus.
May God live in America again.

THE SOLACE OF NIGHT, The International Library of Poetry, 2002

ONLY GOD'S LOVE MAKES THIS DAY POSSIBLE

Cardinals are one of God's most beautiful birds.
Their yearly presence reaffirms
the length, strength and depth of our love.
Bluebirds mating and watching over their young
remind us to care for our sons and daughters
until they can fly.
I pray for our children who have taken flight.
May the Spirit of God soar with their dreams
And aspirations.
May the Son of God lead them toward a caring, sharing
person.
May the glory of God fill their hearts with grace and
compassion.
I praise God for the grandeur
and splendor of sunrise and sunset.
I thank Him for stars at night and
all our flights on a hummingbird's wing.
You are my wife and truly,
the most precious love of my life.
Thirty years have gone by for you and I.
Only God's Love makes this day possible.

AMERICA AT THE MILLENNIUM, The International Library of Poetry, 2000

LAMP OF ETERNAL LIFE

I witnessed your first breath of life
Like Joseph did with God's Son Jesus Christ.
I know, God's greatest Gift on earth
Is the miracle of an infant birth.

Out of the warmth of your mother's womb,
You shivered like Jesus in a cold stone tomb.
Helpless and defenseless you were given to me,
I knew not the future only God could See.

I saw only joy on your mother's face
Like Mary who was filled with His Holy Grace.
The Spirit of God who resides every place,
Entered my heart in that cubicle of space.

I am your father as God is Our Father.
Let us embrace father to mother, sister to brother.
Let us honor each other and His Son Jesus Christ,
A Flame from the Lamp of Eternal Life.

POETRY'S ELITE, The International Library of Poetry, 2001

OLYMPIC PARK

A worm
raised in darkness
tunneled to the surface
and planted a bomb.

The bomb
killed one
and injured a hundred
who caused no harm.

Their cries
and suffering
are the ears and eyes
now searching dirt.

You'll be found,
Pulled out of the ground,
and devoured
like the worm you are.

BEST POEMS OF 1998, The National Library of Poetry, 1998

TAKE ME HOME

I enter a gothic door for the first time,
afraid, apprehensive and heavy of heart.
No one wants to go to or be in a place
where dignity and freedom are lost.
Finality creeps out of halls and walls
as I pass pleading stares and seas of white hair.
This is a prison of aged, worn out flesh,
where Angels and demons battle for souls.

The room I seek now looms before me
And with a quick breath I stepped inside.
Tied to the bed with tubes and needles
Lay the frail old man I came to see.
He clasped his withered hand to mine
And Jesus passed between our lives.
All my sadness now tears of gladness
For God has come to take him home.

A PLEASANT REVERIE, The National Library of Poetry, 1998

WHEN

Parched and thirsty,
Why do you live in a desert?
When Jesus, God's oasis,
Is living water that flows?

Cold and angry,
Why do you shiver and shake?
When Jesus is God's Love,
And Warmth that is forever.

Lonely and empty,
Why are you in the dark?
When Jesus is God's light
And promise of eternal life?

Confused and unsure
Why do you walk the streets?
When Jesus is God's Path
And Jesus is God's Son.

THE INCANDESCENT JUNGLE, The International Library of Poetry, 2001

“Hidden Feelings Die Unspoken” (Revised)

This section contains a revision of my first poetry book published by Watermark Press in 1996. The revision consists of adding published and new unpublished poems to the original work.

Love

SOFTNESS

Softness is the essence
Of my feeling for you.
Were I to paint this delicate thought,
My brush would never touch the canvas.

ALL THAT YOU ARE

To share is to know
Life's touch of soul
And earth's nearest star.
To know is to love
All that you were
And all that you are.

LOVELIEST WOMAN

Loveliest woman
Dreams could ever inspire.
I am, in reality,
One with you,
For you are like a desert oasis
And river swift,
Thoughts could not hold back
Nor thirst refuse.

OUR LOVE

Our love
Is not a memory or point in time,
Place to hide or space to find.

Our love
Is soul and mind entwined,
Within a spectrum yet defined.

FLIRTATION

Eyes met blushing,
Lips wet touching,
Feeling real, on a wheel,
Of thoughts expressed.

LOVE

Enchanted by a lovely lady
Whose alluring beauty drew me near.
I faltered briefly for a moment
And watched the figure disappear.

Magnificent hues of setting sun,
And lustrous glow of ending day.
Could not have made me feel so much,
Nor moved my heart in such a way.

WERE WE TO MEET AGAIN

Were we to meet again,
You having gone your way and I mine,
Would not be as the first,
When sky and stars were ours,
Bound by no one's universe.

We would be older and wiser,
And meet like strangers with refrain.
Yet I, in joy of seeing you,
Would give of heart anew
Were we to meet again.

YOU ARE BUT A DREAM

You are beauty undefined,
flowing from a cup of wine,
which drugs the body and the mind
of a mortal men like me.

The softest words
have not been spoken.
The song of songs
has not been sung.
The greatest poem
remains undone,
for you are but a dream.

You are like a playful breeze,
inviting when you want to tease,
only just to disappear,
when love is offered in return.

The softest words
have not been spoken.
the song of songs
has not been sung.
The greatest poem
remains undone,
for you are but a dream.

KEYSTONE

Air like wine
Wine like air
Share a dream
A dream two share
Climbing heights
Of heights unclimbed
Unending in
A love unending.

HILTON HEAD LOST

With you not there
There was nothing to share
And void became a solitaire.

No words to say
I walked the beach by day
And sifted all the nights away.

I could not see
If landed beauty be
In distant waves upon the sea.

For dye was cast
And time went past
Slowly through an hour glass.

THROUGH THE YEARS

We've laughed a lot and shared some tears.
We've weathered kids and other fears.
It's been fifteen momentous years,
Here's to a bond of love.

Though days and nights will surely pass,
Like sand within an hour glass,
What we have was meant to last,
As I renew my vows.

I love you as I have before.
Tomorrow I will love you more,
For there's no love a heart can't store
For all the years to come,

Nature and Life

AUTUMN'S PRISM

Autumn's Prism
Gleams like jewels
Around your form.
My youthful green
Is lost beneath
Your golden amber.

I love you
As I love the season.

A SUMMER'S STORM

Battle lines were being drawn.
A boisterous wind was first to bellow.
I watched the flowers tremble yellow.

The sky was not to be outdone.
Gird with clouds about her waist,
She shook the ground and all around.

Amused by all the child's play
The mighty sun and last to act,
Beat the sky and pompous wind.

The reddened wind and blackened sky
Cried and howled upon the earth,
And thus began a summer's storm.

BE IT FALL TO CHANGE IT ALL

Colored leaves
released from trees,
Join birds in flight
of warmer nights.
When things go wrong
And life is no song.
Be it fall to change it all.

DAWN

Light of yonder horizon awakens,
The dewy eyed blue bells of morn.

Yawns of beasts and birds in song,
Begin the harmonious concert of dawn.

TILL I AGAIN COULD FEEL THE RAIN

A bolt of lightening
Crackled through a darkened sky,
Landing at my feet so close,
Alarms went off in all directions.
For a second I was dead
And every muscle twitched
Till I again could feel the rain.

SHEILA

You are my first
And need only know.
I love you and will be there
If you are ever in need.

TWINLIGHT

"It's a boy!" he said.
"Thank God!" she said.
"Oh! No!" I said,
As he said, "Wait!"

"Push again!" he said.
"Oh! No!" she said.
"Oh! Yes!" I said,
As he said, "Push!"

"Is it a boy!" she said.
"Oh! Yes!" he said.
"Oh! No!" we said
As he said, "Twins!"

MAKE IT YOUR DAY

A championship hill
Is heart beyond skill
And courage to play.

Work hard as a team,
Live out your dream
And make it your day.

TO A PREGNANT WOMAN

Fear not a child or pain to come.
Fear not the looks or envious smiles.
Fear not your body's growth inside
That's bearing love of life to be.

FLOWERS OF GOD

Flowers of God are;
A child's heart,
A woman's love,
And a friends embrace.

IN MEMORY OF LUCY

Lucy was a special friend.
Her loss was irreplaceable.
How do you replace wit and humor?
How do you replace understanding?
How do you replace a caring person?
She was truly a child of God.

Reflections

TWILIGHT PEACE

Filtered rays through web like clouds
Shroud all wistful gazing eyes.
A weathered fence grown shadow's length
Casts it's spell upon the green.
A willow's pulse of evening breeze
Fans a long perspiring day,
As restful blends of soften light
Bow to eyelids of the night.

WITH OUT A PURPOSE

What is it
that causes one
to turn
against themselves?

What is it
that causes one
to near
the edge of death?

What is it
that causes one
to jump and die?

If not a fear,
within a sphere,
without a purpose?

ONE WAY BUS TO NOWHERE

Running hard and running fast,
They came in from everywhere,
Just to buy a single fare,
On a one way bus to nowhere.
No spoken word, no voice is heard.
No eight to five to stay alive.
No rush to beat the downtown traffic.
Secure at last a frame of mind.
Nothing's on the road ahead.
No one's on the road behind.
One finds only peace of mind
On a one way bus to nowhere.

WHEN NOISES CEASE

Marbled red sinks to bed.
Hazy gray fades away.
There's a peace when noises cease
From children's chatter, lawnmower's clatter
And the neighbors' idle prater.
No more shadows, no more light
Today has slipped into the night.

Lonely stars now drink in bars.
Darkness peers o'er all our fears.
And music plays as noises cease
From children's chatter, lawnmower's clatter
And the neighbors' idle prater.
Burning souls that drain martinis,
Toast the night's finite linguini.

Tomorrow breaks and brightness wakes
Anchored eyes avoiding skies,
Where dreams of peace and noises cease
From children's chatter, lawnmower's clatter
And the neighbors' idle prater.
Again the day awaits the night
Like tallow spend from candlelight.

DEEP DOWN WE HAVE A SOUL

Deep down we have a soul
Where all emotions go
Seeking inner sanctum
From pressure of without
And pressure from within.
Let it be love were it to overflow.

WAILING IN THE WILDERNESS

I am but a particle of dust
Blown about a dirt-filled earth,
Quivering like the minute ripples
Flushing out the oceans bowels.

I am but a ram confused
Mired in the dug of pleasure,
Spread across the fields of grass
Like honey on a child's tongue.

I am but a fly unwary
Pinned beneath a swatter grinning,
Squashed and squirming in a mix
Of breathless blood and beadless sweat.

I am but a leper's flesh
Decadent and loose of limb,
Hanging like an anguished aura
Drawing quick the maggot's mouth.

I am but an aspen dying
Stripped of autumn's brazen colors,
Clutching cold and barren branches
Frosted by the chill of death.

Wailing In The Wilderness.

A POET' STEAD

Sadness is a poet's stead,
By weight of all the verse I've read.
Who buys or eats of bitter bread
Or seeks the sadness I have read.

UNFILLED DREAMS

Nights on end upon a chair,
I search and seek a solitaire.
Lost it seems,
Upon a shelf of unfilled dreams.

AN AWESOME THOUGHT

Heaven, earth or universe
Need but flicker,
And I, a fragile frame,
Would a mound of ashes be.

UNTITLED

The intersect of dusk and dawn
Cools the night and heats the day.
The apex of the moon and sun
Heightens dreams and aspirations.
We are points upon life's graph
Awaiting crossroads yet to come.

UNTITLED

Those who come
in God's name,
May rule nations
but not human beings.
Who have survived
all these years,
Believing life
is a sacred right.

THE HIVE

A door knob clicks.
One by one they enter in.
Soon the room is filled with hums.
The waltz of drones has now begun.
Single sounds are drowned out
By endless waves of hum, hum, hum.

FIFTY-FIVE

Tomorrow I'll be fifty-five.
By the grace of God I'm still alive.
When Jesus puts my soul to sleep,
My toil on earth will be complete.

A SONNET TO A BROTHER-IN-LAW

Twenty-six years ago we met.
To this day I feel your compassionate heart.
Though a generation apart,
I knew from the start we were kindred spirits.

Fathers recognize fathers
Who do more with less than most would endure.
Surely we have a passion for life
For we dearly love our children and wife.

We've made our share of mistakes
Each and every day along the way
And our heart breaks when our mistakes
Become the only mirror of our reflection.

Poor in spirit, gentle and kind
God's Son will find your compassionate heart.

ONE AMONG US

Today is a day to glorify and praise God
For one among us has been a faithful servant.
With hard work, he served his colleagues.
With honor, he served God and country.
With love, he has served his wife and children.
Today is truly a day of joy and celebration.

Faith

GOD LOVES ME AND GOD LOVES YOU

each day i awake and breath i take
is a Gift from God who loves me

i need only open my ears and eyes
to recognize my Heavenly Father

i need only open my heart and soul
to feel the warmth of His Embrace

God loves me and God loves you,
an awesome, joyous, spiritual truth.

AT JOURNEY'S END

Leaves of trees bed a man
Who dared trek through life's vast forest.
A pure and crystal mountain stream,
Bathes and cleans his tired feet.

A Living Breeze, with light caress,
Relieves his pain and loneliness,
As nature's sound, from all around,
Softly lulls his heart to sleep.

WHEN MY GOD IS NEAR

When my God is near,
The sweetest voice I hear,
Whispers in my ear
To free me from all fear.

A PRAYER TO GOD

My one
And only prayer,
Is God
In my life forever.

A FALLEN CROWN

A drunkard drinking
Saw the mob and weighted figure
Heading toward Golgotha, and said
"What hath he done?"

The crowd in laughter
Spat upon his face, and jeered
"Make way, make way, ye fool of fools,
Lest ye replace the king of kings."

Daring not the multitude
He hid within a bitter wine,
As all went forth
To witness yet another death.

Hours later when all had gone
He wept before the dying man, who said
"Father forgive them
For they know not what they do."

Then darkness swallowed darkness.
The man upon the cross was dead.
How earth did quake and shake
As saints arose from opened graves.

Then God knelt down,
Setting sky and earth ablaze,
To gather in His precious Son
And fallen crown.

TRILOGY OF GRIEF

In The Parlor	I saw death Cold and proud Finely dressed Lying in a velvet box I saw not my father.
In The Church	I saw Jesus Flowing warmly From all songs And prayers expressed And freely wept As He knelt down To wash and cleanse My father's feet.
In The Field	I saw honor In the faces Of those who braved A cold and chilling Winter's wind To share my grief Now sealed within My father's grave God Rest His Soul.

TAKE CARE OF MY CHILDREN

Before a newborn ever cries,
Life in your body lives or dies.
What you do to this child,
You do to God.

When you hear a helpless cry,
Hold and dry an infant's eyes.
The love you give to them,
You give to God.

If a child is having trouble,
Help them in their time of need.
The care you give to them,
God will give tenfold.

THE LIGHT AND THE WAY

God is eternal,
Believe in Him.
His Spirit will
Live in you.
This is the Light!

God is redeeming.
Embrace His Son.
His Love will
Fill your soul.
This is the Way!

THE SECOND COMING

A cosmic stream descends
To gather Clovites few in number.
As Amorics and Shebedons
Bathe in lust and drink clarventum.

The end is near
And Cloviterus
Once crushed upon the stone of Shill
Now stands before God's mighty Army.

DO NOT FEED THE BEAST

Woe unto the man who feeds the Beast
For the Beast will consume your soul.
No riches, power or illumination on earth
Will escape the Wrath of God.

JUDGMENT OF THE ANTI-CHRIST

Those who feed on human misery,
Profit in the name of God
Or deliberately destroy His Creation
Cease to exist in the Final Judgment.

PREPARE THE MASTER'S WAY

I have seen Good and Evil,
Raging in the sky,
Silenced by the Hand of God.
I have seen lighting white
His Thunder Snow
Strike and chill the earth.
I have seen His awesome power
Eclipse the sun and moon.
I have seen the Holy Star,
Prepare the Master's Way.

TURN ON GOD'S LIGHT

When you are troubled
And can't sleep at night,
Pick up a Bible
And turn on God's Light.

When you're awake
And can't face the day,
Sum up the courage
And reason to pray.

When you're alone
Thinking nobody cares,
Reach out to God
Who will always be there.

If you have lost it
And have nowhere to go,
Turn on God's Light
And empty your soul.

WEARY FEET

In the next millennium,
We will be humbled by God.
Jesus will walk the streets.
Anointing the souls of weary feet.

Celebration

A BETHLEHEM STAR

On a clear and crystal night
I saw it in the sky
The brightest of the heavenly stars
Wondrous to the eye.
Glowing like a coal afire
Spreading love and joy abound
Just as it did so long ago
In the town where Christ was found.
I in awe took in it's splendor
Praising God who caused to be
This sign of everlasting life
And light for all the world to see.

THE CHRISTMAS CAT

There he sat, the Christmas Cat watching snowflakes fall.
Let outside, he pranced and danced at all the wetness on his paws.
Alert, awake, with perfect sight, he didn't catch a single flake.
Wet and cold, he came inside and snoozed away a trying day.

I later spied the Christmas Cat beneath a lighted tree.
Content to lie, sometimes he'd play while purring oh so noisily.
From time to time, he'd stretch and yawn to Jingle Bells or Tannenbaum.
He'd swat the tinsel to and fro, or try to untie another bow.

There he lay, the Christmas Cat late on Christmas Eve.
No one about, with all lights out, he quickly went to sleep.
Santa grinned from ear to ear, no Christmas cat would catch him here.
He laid a ball between his paws, just before he disappeared.

I watched him stretch, the Christmas Cat early Christmas morn.
He sniffed the ball, rolled it down the hall and batted it all around.
What a day and feast it was, a goose was cooked, he ate of that,
Then curled up and went to sleep, one contented Christmas cat.

THAT'S WHAT IT'S ALL ABOUT

Bells are ringing.
Angels are singing.
Christ was born
On Christmas morning,
Give of heart
To all mankind.

Children are laughing.
Mischief is brewing.
Bless the hope
And joy they bring,
In remembrance
Of our King.

To share is to give.
To love is to live.
And that's what it's all about.

Lights are shining.
Fires are burning.
Warmth and glow
Greet all who enter.
Let all come
Who wish to share.

Goodies are baking.
Dinner is cooking.
Set a table
For your loved ones,
And another
In His name.

To share is to give.
To love is to live.
And that's what it's all about.

A tree is glowing,
Gifts overflowing.
There's a happiness
In knowing,
Someone's there
And someone cares.

Music is playing.
Everyone's dancing.
God bless all
Who've come together
To celebrate
His Holy Son.

To share is to give.
To love is to live.
And that's what it's all about.

NEW YEAR'S EVE

A warm embrace,
A kiss of sweetness
Toast a crystal glass held high,

A bond renewed,
A light of love
Reflect upon the sparkling wine.

A new resolve,
A sense of strength
Kindle flames of brighter fires.

A CHRISTMAS THOUGHT

On the freeway miles of cars,
There's no space in stores or bars,
Angry faces push and shove,
What happened to an ounce of love?
How will Santa find his way,
The grinch stole all the lights, the say.
No Christmas lights except for stars
And candles in the heart of ours.
Let's look within this Christmastide,
For there is where our love resides.
A radiant warmth for winter nights.
More precious than the glowing lights.

MISTLETOE

On Christmas Eve
I knelt before a candle lit,
To lowly branches of mesquite
Bearing fruit of love abundant.

CHRISTMAS

How time seems to pass
As we become older,
Wiser, and closer in spirit.
Christmas
More than any other time,
I count my many blessings
And extend them to you,
My closest and dearest of friends.

CHRISTMAS 1984

Charity, and act of good will
Hallows the hope God gave mankind.
Remembrance of God's Son
Inspires and touches hearts of us all.
Sharing, if but for a moment
With family and friends
Encompasses the meaning of Christmas.
Christmas is inspiration and understanding
Sanctified by the glory of God.

A CHRISTMAS CANDLE

On Christmas Eve
My daughter and I
Lit a candle
Outside our door
In a paper bag.

"How will it burn"
She said,
"When it's so cold"
"With love," I said
As we looked out to see.

WE BELIEVE IN CHRISTMAS

As we gather around a tree,
As we raise our voices high,
As we kneel on bended knee,
Bless us all!
In giving what we have to give,
For we believe in Christmas.

LET US BE ONE

Let us be one,
Caring where we have not cared,
Giving where we have not given,
Sharing where we have not shared,
Reaching where we have not reached,
For Christmas nineteen eighty-one.

JESUS THIS CHRISTMAS

Dear God I pray for our sons and daughters
Who have rejected Your Son and Holy Spirit.

I pray for all men and women on earth
Who are defending and spreading Your Word.

I pray for victims of September Eleventh,
Swept away by evil, now in Your Care.

I pray for the poor, the sick and the suffering
And for earthly saints who attend them.

Dear God I humbly pray for all of us
For we truly need Jesus this Christmas.

IT' CHRISTMAS IN AMERICA

Lights like celestial stars
Shine across our nation.
Voices raised is praise
Fill the air with gladness.
Children sing and Church bells ring
It's Christmas in America.

HALLELUJAH, AMEN

Twenty-seven years
All joy and few tears,
Love ever flowing,
Growing and glowing,
Soul mates we,
Seeds of God's Tree,
One humble story,
Of God's Great Glory,

Hallelujah, Amen.

I TRULY LOVE YOU

I have loved you for awhile,
Yet we are but a ripple in a pond.
The wider and further we go
The more I know I truly love you.